Stockworth

An American CEO

Hinda Sterling and Herb Selesnick

Abt Books • Cambridge, Massachusetts

Library of Congress Cataloging-in-Publication Data
Sterling, Hinda
Stockworth: An American CEO
1. Chief Executive officers — United States — Caricatures and cartoons.
2. Executives — United States — Caricatures and cartoons.
3. American wit and humor, Pictorial.
I. Selesnick, Herb. II. Title.
PN6727.S694S76 1989   741.5′973   88-7458
ISBN 0-89011-600-8

Printed in the United States of America

For our parents

Cast of Characters

Stockworth's principal characters surrounding personnel manager Polly Nurture seated, clockwise from bottom left: executive assistant Libby Sloan, shipping foreman Upton Downs, executive secretary Mary Scuttle, chairman Seymour Stockworth, marketing vice president Ernest Hopeful, treasurer Audie McBean, and junior executive Bif Gambit

Contents

Introduction

We like to draw and write about executives. Since we make our living as management consultants, perhaps it's natural that we would find humor among the people with whom we work. Observing how they live, think and behave has always been the most engaging form of business analysis for us, more interesting by far than market research, industry profiles or even our own personnel studies. We hope you share our relish for executive watching, and that the pages that follow will tickle your vanity by affirming your own perceptions.

We created *Stockworth* to fill an important void in contemporary American fiction.* At a time when economic and business affairs dominate the news and appear increasingly to shape the national character, it is truly remarkable how small a segment of American art, entertainment and literature deals with the executive suite or the boardroom. And yet these are the areas in which the power of money and the workings of ego and ambition connect and reverberate with millions of lives and trillions of dollars.

More than 40 million Americans have money invested in the stock market. Fifteen million college-educated professionals manage the companies in which they have invested. Two out of every three Americans are employed in the private sector. Business accounts for about 80 percent of the national income and, through taxes and contributions, makes possible most of the other ventures that comprise our national life.

Like sports fans, those who are directly involved with the business world hungrily devour the latest reports and statistics abundantly available in newspapers and magazines. Business students, of whom there are a growing number, eagerly tackle the subject matter of their textbooks, of which there are an even faster growing number. The managerial and financial professions have been engulfed by a wave of prosperity never seen before.

Yet, in spite of all this, business as a dramatic human enterprise, capable of evoking the good, the bad and the comical, is seldom a world we read about. Wait for a business novel from Mailer, Bellow or Roth and you might wait forever, while John Updike's *Rabbit Is Rich* and Tom Wolfe's *The Bonfire of the Vanities* are at best peripheral to the world of business. On Broadway, it is a long leap in time from Arthur Miller's *All My Sons* and *Death of a Salesman* or Abe Burroughs' *How to Succeed in Business Without Really Trying,* none of which is really about business, to David Mamet's *American Buffalo* and *Glengarry Glen Ross,* both of which really are. From Hollywood (dismissing *Silkwood, The China Syndrome, Rollover* and *Wall Street*), there simply are no candidates, serious or otherwise.

Businessmen and women on commercial television typically are caricaturized as crooks, con artists, lost souls or, in the words of EG&G Chairman Bernard J. O'Keefe, "greedy people who shout all the time." *Dallas* and *Dynasty* offer at best occasional snapshots of large glass office buildings with the focus on a charming scoundrel, J.R. Ewing, or a vengeful and destructive Alexis Carrington.

Some years back, writers such as Cameron Hawley and Sloan Wilson gave us business novels like *Executive Suite, Cash McCall* and *The Man in the Gray*

---

* The ideas in this introduction and much of our thinking about *Stockworth* have been shaped by Michael M. Thomas ("Tough Times for the Financial Fiction Novel," *The New York Times,* October 20, 1986, Section VI, pp. 43–59; Eric Sevareid (introduction to *Enterprise: The Making of Business in America,* McGraw-Hill, 1983); Eric Pace ("The Businessman as Villain," *The New York Times,* April 15, 1984, p. F15); and by introductory commentaries from William F. Buckley, Jr., John Kenneth Galbraith, Garry Wills and Charles Saxon (in *Doonesbury's Greatest Hits* by G.B. Trudeau, Holt, Rinehart and Winston, 1978; *Money Should Be Fun* by William Hamilton, Houghton Mifflin, 1980; *The Doonesbury Chronicles* by G.B. Trudeau, Holt, Rinehart and Winston, 1975; and *Honesty Is One of the Better Policies* by Charles Saxon, Viking Press, 1984.)

Flannel Suit. But recently, other than the efforts of Earl Norris and the late L.E. Sissman and John P. Marquand, little on the subject of business has been produced. Nothing exists for business that is comparable, for example, with writer-lawyer Louis Auchincloss's fictionalized treatment of the marvelously rich and tensioned office lives within law firms.

Business as a genuine exploring ground for art and fiction has largely been ignored in the last twenty years. But it wasn't always thus. The interaction between human character and business institutions has engaged novelists from Jane Austen on. For example, the organized making of money was a central concern of the works of Balzac, Dickens and Trollope. Interestingly, the best, most lasting work of these writers was done during commerce-driven times not unlike our own.

The industrialization of 19th-century England was a fertile breeding ground for speculators, promoters and others obsessed with various forms of acquisitiveness. Hence, Dickens' Scrooge, Ralph Nickleby and Merdie in *Little Dorrit,* his use of the details of scams to capture the reader's attention (the Great Metropolitan Muffin and Crumpet Company in *Nicholas Nickleby,* the railway swindle in *Martin Chuzzlewit*) and Trollope's Augustus Melmotte in *The Way We Live Now.* The ascendent French bourgeoisie during this same period were well along in the process of wedding commercial gain with social advancement, arguably Balzac's great subject.

The equivalent American conviction that business success opened the way to the best table in town was documented and interpreted by Dreiser in *The Financier, The Titan* and *The Stoic,* by Edith Wharton and later by Sinclair Lewis. In fact, American literature had a rich albeit brief tradition of business fiction.

Novelists in addition to Dreiser, Wharton and Lewis on this side of the Atlantic who were centrally concerned with the businessman have included Henry James, William Dean Howells, Frank Norris, Jack London, David Graham Phillips, Robert Herrick, Upton Sinclair, Ernest Poole and Booth Tarkington. James, Howells and Tarkington all found in the businessman many of the enduring American virtues. For the rest of these writers, however, the business world was savagely competitive, brutally aggressive and ethically corrupt. Their novels, generally speaking, are solemn or grandly melodramatic denunciations of monstrous figures of aggressive evil who are motivated solely by money, power and prestige.

The businessman in American fiction before the First World War was the tycoon, the powerful manufacturer, the vast speculator, the fabulous financier, the monarch of enormous enterprises, the arch-individual responsible only to himself. His concern was with production.

The tycoon may still have been the most colorful and dramatic figure in the American business myth after 1918, but he was no longer by any means the characteristic figure in American business fiction. Sinclair Lewis, with his portrait of George F. Babbitt, a conniving, prosperous real estate man, created in 1922 one of the ugliest but most convincing figures in American fiction—the total conformist. *Babbitt* and some of Lewis's other novels satirize the world of small businessmen and, more particularly, of middlemen—portraying them as a crowd of ninnies and buffoons who, if they are malicious and mean, are also ridiculous and even pathetic. Not in the least resembling 19th century autocratic individuals, Lewis's businessmen are compromising conformists whose moral defections are anything but spectacular. No producers themselves, their success depends on public relations, in the pursuit of which they diminish human relations and, finally, their own humanity.

Daddy Warbucks in the *Little Orphan Annie* comic strip and Mr. Dithers in the *Blondie* comic strip are business characters in the entertainment realm who rose to the top of the charts during the 1920s and 1930s respectively. Warbucks, a benevolent munitions tycoon in the pre-World War I mold, whose actions refuted the unpleasant connotations of his name, is probably the only war profiteer ever elevated to hero status in literature. He evolved from a henpecked member of the idle rich (his wife disappeared from the strip soon after its 1924 inception) to foster father, adventurous soldier of fortune, international businessman and, ultimately, the richest man in the world. Co-stars of one of the five top comic strips for decades, Annie and Daddy Warbucks were the basis for a long-running radio serial, a hit Broadway musical and three movies.

A worldwide audience of nearly 250 million devoted daily newspaper readers instantly recognize not only Blondie and Dagwood Bumstead, lead characters of the *Blondie* comic strip, but also Dagwood's crochety old boss, Mr. Dithers, who has rehired Dagwood as many times as he has fired him.

In contrast with these earlier efforts, no writer of serious or humorous fiction has emerged in recent years who has dealt successfully with the money side of modern life. No business novel has captured the attention of those who look to fiction to reveal the underlying themes of life. Nor has one aroused the enthusiasms of the general audience which reads fiction principally to be entertained.

Hence, *Stockworth: An American CEO.* When we first started doing an ensemble-style business comic strip for the stock market page of the *Boston Globe,* the paper's business editor, Gordon McKibben, and his associate, John Robinson, after studying the new feature for a few weeks, announced virtually in unison: "Your best character is the board chairman; I feel like I *know* him!" Never ones to ignore a client cue, we switched gears and proceeded to focus the strip on a middle-aged self-content corporate chieftain named Seymour Stockworth. Other subcategories of businessmen and women certainly found their way into the strip during its 1982–1986 national syndication run but, with a salute to our first editors and valued supporters, the strip remained focused on chairman Stockworth, as is this collection.

Why a comic strip? The business of America may not be solely business, as Calvin Coolidge once said, but much of what is truly engaging about the national character is to be found in the delicious irony of American business manners. For proof of this contention, one has only to look at *The Wall Street Journal*'s daily business cartoon, *Pepper...and Salt* which, according to the *Journal*'s own statistics, is among the paper's most frequently read features (read even more often than the stock market prices themselves!). In fact, newspaper surveys consistently show comics of all kinds to be at the very top in readership, often over even front-page stories. Not since the 1920s, however, has a newspaper comic been built around the character and values of a business person. We designed *Stockworth* to fill this void at a time, in the early 1980s, when business values were, if not ascendant, then certainly resurgent.

We followed our muse into the realm of daily comic strips in an effort to compete more effectively for limited reader attention in an age of 30-second TV sound bites. How, after all, can business fiction match the real-life stories of, say, Ivan Boesky or Armand Hammer, the soap operas of the Gettys and the Hunts, John DeLorean's misadventures, or the Begelman affair? How can anyone manufacture characters as colorful as 1980s executive celebrities Donald Trump, Rupert Murdoch, Ted Turner, T. Boone Pickens, Carl Icahn, Robert Vesco or Lee Iacocca? To us, the answer seemed clear: Be brief. Be graphic. And be funny.

We also wanted to redress what we saw as an imbalance in the treatment of business in syndicated comics. With the exception of the aforementioned *Pepper...and Salt* and an occasional William Hamilton or Charles Saxon cartoon, before *Stockworth* came on the scene so-called business comics offered only negative stereotypes: either the greedy, pompous or intimidating boss, or the powerless worker trapped in the dehumanizing grip of a mindless bureaucracy. The standard journalistic defense for this stereotyping was that a kindly boss who always operates in a highly ethical fashion would *not* be amusing, that the primary function of comic strips is to entertain, and that comics are not intended to provide real life views of people. To be sure, this defense had begun to wear thin in the face of increasing readership objections to negative stereotyping of females, minorities, the elderly and the handicapped in some traditional comics. More recently, it has been all but demolished with the spectacular emergence of cartoon realism in the work of Jules Feiffer and Garry Trudeau.

Stockworth is in this realist mode. It offers a broad picture of chairman Seymour Stockworth's lifestyle and values as well as some of the more humanizing details of his daily existence. The comic strip depicts Stockworth as one of the 1980s breed of successful, dedicated, self-aware CEOs. He probably grew up during the Depression, so he is pragmatic and cares about dollars and sense. He matured during World War II and the 1950s, a period of unquestioned American dominance, so he is self-consciously power oriented. He formed his professional aspirations when business publicly initiated many social reforms, so he is more public and candidly expressive than his board room predecessors.

The mechanics of the comic-strip genre dictate a choice of whether to reintroduce the reader to the point in the story at which he was dropped by the artist the day before (a continuity strip) or make each daily offering more or less free-standing (a gag strip). We chose the latter form, which then posed the requirement of a genuine laugh (or at least a wry chuckle) in the ultimate panel of each strip. This task no artist can hope to fulfill with wholly satisfying consistency, although we must all try. A collection runs the risk of highlighting the unevenness by inviting assessments of which strips are "the funniest." There is also the compression of the comic strip form. In a collection, this is more nettlesome than if twenty-four hours have gone by between readings. (*Warning:* for best results, ingest the material in this book in small periodic doses.)

There were physical changes in *Stockworth* over the period of time from which these strips were drawn. Some changes were deliberate, others were utterly unconscious. Sometimes they may leap out at you when one strip is juxtaposed with another drawn two years earlier or later.

The cartooning devices we used to cope with these mechanical limitations—extended narratives that make their own complexity the starting point for humor, repeated panels with little or no visual change to indicate thought processes going on behind a facade, recurring scenes and subjects to build texture and themes "pointillistically," the well-tailored but underexercised and somewhat overfed bodies exuding superb contentment and satisfaction with self—all serve to show just how much we have learned from and are indebted to Hamilton, Saxon, Feiffer and Trudeau.

Today, both genders, all ethnic groups and a growing number of foreign nationals are part of this country's executive mainstream. As a result, many business leaders no longer resemble the Stockworth club-type executive. The strip made no effort to capture these developments. We are not social historians. Our purpose was to mirror the life of one contemporary executive subspecies. Neither are we satirists. When we were doing the strip, we felt an empathy for Stockworth. We tried to portray him honestly.

Whatever success we may have had is due in no small measure to the advice and encouragement received from Sam Summerlin and Paula Reichler of the New York Times Syndication Sales Corporation and to the editors who chose to place *Stockworth* in over seventy publications with more than eight million readers in the United States, Great Britain and the Far East. The quality and comprehensiveness of this collection are a credit to Clark Abt's curatorial sensibility and the hard work of Kay Hardy, Vicki Levin and Sally MacGillivray. Lastly, we are indebted to our family, friends and clients for indulging us good-naturedly while we descended into the basement of our home for the better part of four years to free-associate on chairmanly ways.

Beverly Cove
March 1989

Running the Show

3

Solving Problems

8

12

Perks

Ego

Ups and Downs

THE STOCK MARKET SURGED AHEAD LAST WEEK.

INVESTORS SCRAMBLED. TRADING SIZZLED.

VOLUME SWELLED. THE DOW SOARED.

IT WAS A PRETTY GOOD WEEK.

IT WAS A TURBULENT WEEK FOR COMMODITIES.

CATTLE SLUMPED. PORK BELLIES FROZE. THERE WERE PRESSURES IN THE HOG PITS.

COFFEE SOURED. CORN WENT FLAT. SOYBEANS SETTLED SHARPLY LOWER.

RYE OFFERED SOME RELIEF.

THE BOND MARKET TURNED VOLATILE LAST WEEK.

GOOD INFLATION NUMBERS PROVIDED THE STIMULUS, MASSIVE TREASURY BORROWING THE DEPRESSANT.

MARKET ENTHUSIASM WAS TEMPERED BY LOWER YIELD LEVELS, WHILE A SLOWING ECONOMY CREATED NERVOUS TREMORS.

STANDARD & POOR'S WAS MOODY.

28

The Old-Boy Network

Stockholders

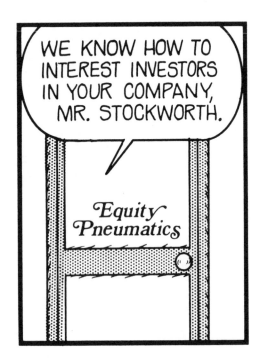

40

Takeovers

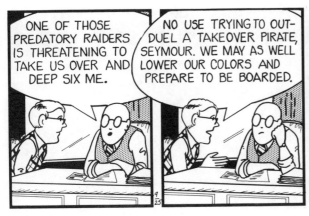

The Media

IS IT TRUE YOUR FIRM'S NEGOTIATING WITH A COMPANY THAT WANTS TO TAKE IT OVER?

NO ASSURANCE CAN BE GIVEN THAT SUCH A TRANSACTION WILL BE CONTEMPLATED OR CONSUMMATED.

I'M CONFUSED.

I THOUGHT I RECOGNIZED YOUR VOICE.

ON THIS INVESTIGATIVE REPORT I'M DOING ABOUT YOUR INDUSTRY, MR. STOCKWORTH...

I'M TRYING TO DIG AS DEEP AS I CAN.

YOU'VE GOTTEN PRETTY LOW.

I'M WILLING TO GO WHERE MY STORY LEADS ME.

WE HOPE YOU WILL.

IS IT TRUE THAT YOU ALONE SPEAK FOR YOUR COMPANY?

THAT ANYONE WHO TALKS TO THE PRESS WITHOUT PERMISSION INCURS YOUR WRATH?

ABSOLUTELY NOT.

BY THE WAY, WHO TOLD YOU THAT?

Leadership

Cleaning House

Keeping Score

81

85

Corporate Finance

BUT ALL WE'RE ASKING FOR IS $20 MILLION...

MR. STOCKWORTH, THIS LENDING INSTITUTION IS NOT A BOTTOMLESS WELL OF FINANCING.

IF WE TURN YOU DOWN, WILL YOU STILL BE MY GUEST FOR LUNCH?

ONLY IF I CAN HAVE A LITTLE WHINE.

I WAS AFRAID YOU'D TURN US DOWN BECAUSE WE ALREADY OWE SO MUCH.

BUT YOU APPROVED OUR LOAN ANYWAY.

NOW HOW DO YOU FEEL?·

DEEPLY INDEBTED.

OUR PHILOSOPHY IS TO HAVE AS LITTLE DEBT AS POSSIBLE...

SO HOW COME WE OWE SO MUCH?

1984 BORROWING

"POSSIBLE" IS A KEY WORD HERE...

WE'RE HOPING YOUR INVESTMENT BANK WILL UNDERWRITE A BOND ISSUE FOR US.

UNFORTUNATELY, OUR DEBT RATING IS ONLY TRIPLE B.

WHY HAVE YOU COME TO US?

WE HEARD YOU HANDLE JUNK BONDS.

WE CALL THEM "PROBLEM LOANS."

I UNDERSTAND. DAD WAS IN "SALVAGE."

WE'D LIKE TO SELL $200 MILLION OF COMMERCIAL PAPER ON THE CHEAP.

PERHAPS YOU SHOULD COLLATERALIZE IT.

IF THERE'S A DEFAULT, WHAT WOULD YOU BE PREPARED TO LIQUIDATE?

OUR TREASURER.

Competition

WE SHOULD HAVE OUR CUSTOMERS SIGN A NONDISCLOSURE AGREEMENT.

WE DON'T WANT THEM GIVING OUR PRODUCT INFORMATION TO THE RUSSIANS.

WE'RE NOT A HIGH TECHNOLOGY FIRM, AUDIE.

WE DON'T WANT THAT TO GET OUT EITHER.

WHAT'S NEW ON THE LOADING DOCK, UPTON? I'M WORRIED ABOUT OUR GARBAGE.

SOME SNOOP COULD STEAL THE TRASH AND SELL OUR BUSINESS SECRETS TO THE HIGHEST BIDDER.

WE SHOULD STATION A NIGHT WATCHMAN INSIDE OUR DUMPSTER, SEYMOUR.

IF IT WEREN'T FOR MY ALLERGIES, I'D GLADLY TAKE THE FIRST SHIFT.

THE INDUSTRIAL SPY CHASER HAS A QUESTION

HOW ROUGH DO YOU WANT ME TO GET?

USE THE WEAPONS OF MODERN CORPORATE WARFARE

...BUT I'M NOT TRAINED IN BLUSTER AND INTIMIDATION

Winning Customers

WHY ARE WE MEETING WITH THIS PROSPECT?

WE BOTH KNOW HE'S NOT READY TO BUY...

NIBBLES MEAN A LOT WHEN YOU'RE FISHING...

HOW MANY TIMES CAN WE TAKE HIM TO LUNCH?

SALES ARE OFF...

WHAT'LL IT TAKE TO TURN THINGS AROUND?

I'D LIKE TO REPLACE THE NATIONAL SALES MANAGER

GOOD OF YOU TO VOLUNTEER,...

OUR MANAGERS ARE OUT OF TOUCH WITH OUR SALESPEOPLE

OUR SALESPEOPLE ARE OUT OF TOUCH WITH OUR CUSTOMERS

AND I WANT TO KNOW WHY

I'LL GET IN TOUCH WITH THEM...

Marketing

106

More Marketing

116

117

Self-Improvement

Organizational Climate

126

Labor Relations

129

133

Executive Search

143

Mentoring

148

155

Deadwood

159

Consultants

164

165

167

168

171

Success

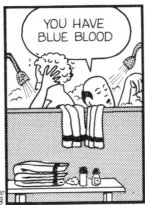

174

More Ups and Downs

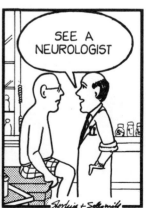

OUR PENSION FUND IS GROWING FASTER THAN WE ARE!

I KNOW

WHAT DO YOU PLAN TO DO ABOUT IT?

RETIRE

MOST CONSERVATIVE BUSINESSMAN I EVER MET...

A RELENTLESS BEAR...

EVEN HIS LAST WISH...

"AVOID THE DOWNSIDE RISK"
FRANK SMITH
R.I.P.

Planned Giving

HEY BUDDY, CAN YOU SPARE SOME CHANGE?

GIVE A MAN MONEY AND FEED HIS FAMILY FOR A DAY...

... GIVE A MAN A JOB AND FEED HIS FAMILY FOR A LIFETIME!

GIVE THIS MAN A QUARTER AND FEED HIS METER FOR AN HOUR

Dear Santa, my name is Seymour Stockworth.

I am 59 years old and chairman of Stockworth Limited.

This year I acquired a hot growth company, sold off some losing subsidiaries and doubled our stock value.

I was real good.

Since your last visit, Santa, the board voted me a big bonus.

I used it to buy everything that was on my list.

I hope you'll still drop by to chit-chat.

We can talk about income averaging.

193

194

Executive Status

THE PRESIDENT HAS TO FILL A TOUGH REGULATORY JOB

WHY DID HE SEND FOR YOU?

PROBABLY MY REPUTATION FOR CALLING THINGS AS I SEE THEM

...SO WHO DO YOU RECOMMEND?

THE PRESIDENT HAS INVITED ME TO THE WHITE HOUSE

HE PROBABLY WANTS MY ADVICE ON TAX REFORM AND THE BUDGET DEFICIT

...OR MAYBE MY VIEWS ON INTERNATIONAL TRADE POLICY

WHO PREPS YOU FOR YOUR TV COMMERCIALS?

MR. PRESIDENT, THE UNION CHIEF I DEAL WITH IS SO GOOD AT HIS JOB...

...I'D LIKE TO SEE HIM BECOME A GOVERNMENT NEGOTIATOR

FOR WHAT?

THE REST OF HIS LIFE!

201

Public Speaking

Family Life

216

Accountability

IT'S FROM THE BOARD OF DIRECTORS.

"YOU SHOULD HAVE AN OUTSIDE INTEREST, SO WE BOUGHT YOU THIS."

ANY REPLY?

A HEARTY THANKS... FROM ONE WHO ISN'T THAT EASILY MOVED.

CHAIRING THIS BOARD GIVES ME THE CHANCE TO PROPOSE GOALS...

SUGGEST STRATEGIES,...

OUTLINE TACTICS,...

...AND ASSIGN YOUR PARKING SPACES

AS THE COMPANY'S TOP MANAGER, I'M HONORED TO CHAIR THIS DISTINGUISHED BOARD...

THE PREVENTION OF FLAGRANT ABUSES OF POWER BY MANAGEMENT IS YOUR JOB.

WHAT IS THE DEFINITION OF "FLAGRANT"?

MY JOB

A Larger Purpose

About the Authors

Hinda Sterling and Herb Selesnick are senior partners of Sterling & Selesnick, Inc., a Massachusetts firm that provides management consulting services for industry and government. Their clients include chief executives and senior officers of major American corporations, federal and state agencies, advanced educational institutions and international professional societies. Hinda Sterling earned degrees in English, graphics and print making from the University of Massachusetts and Pratt Institute. Her artwork appears in management training films used worldwide. Herb Selesnick holds MIT degrees in physics, management and political science. He has written numerous books and articles on management and public policy. More than one hundred organizations have invited Sterling and Selesnick into their board rooms and executive offices to talk about the humorous side of enterprise and other, more sobering aspects of management.

Other Abt Books on Management

The Strategy of Japanese Business by James Abegglen (1979)

Henderson on Corporate Strategy by Bruce Henderson (1984)

The Logic of Business Strategy by Bruce Henderson (1987)

LeBaron on Investment Strategy by Dean LeBaron (1989)

Orbital Management: Beyond the Hierarchy by Jay Lehr (1984)

Winning the Marketing War by Gerald Michaelson (1987)